*f*P

Also by Stephen R. Covey

The 3rd Alternative
The 8th Habit
The Leader in Me
The 7 Habits of Highly Effective People
Predictable Results in Unpredictable Times
Great Work, Great Career
The 7 Habits of Highly Effective Families
Living the 7 Habits
The Nature of Leadership
First Things First
Principle-Centered Leadership

THE
WISDOM
AND TEACHINGS
OF
STEPHEN R. COVEY

FREE PRESS

New York   London   Toronto   Sydney   New Delhi

FREE PRESS
A Division of Simon & Schuster, Inc.
1230 Avenue of the Americas
New York, NY 10020

First Free Press hardcover edition November 2012

FREE PRESS and colophon are trademarks of Simon & Schuster, Inc.

For information about special discounts for bulk purchases,
please contact Simon & Schuster Special Sales at 1-866-506-1949
or business@simonandschuster.com.

The Simon & Schuster Speakers Bureau can bring authors to your live event.
For more information or to book an event, contact the Simon & Schuster Speakers
Bureau at 1-866-248-3049 or visit our website at www.simonspeakers.com.

DESIGNED BY ERICH HOBBING

Manufactured in the United States of America

1   3   5   7   9   10   8   6   4   2

Library of Congress Cataloging-in-Publication Data
Covey, Stephen R.
The wisdom and teachings of Stephen R. Covey.
p. cm.
1. Self-actualization (Psychology) 2. Success—Psychological aspects.
3. Conduct of life. 4. Leadership. I. Title.
BF637.S4C693 2012
158—dc23
2012037290

ISBN 978-1-4767-2511-6
ISBN 978-1-4767-2513-0 (ebook)

CONTENTS

CONTENTS

THE
WISDOM
AND TEACHINGS
OF
STEPHEN R. COVEY

INTRODUCTION

This book contains the crystallized wisdom of one of the great teachers of our time, Dr. Stephen R. Covey.

As a young man, Dr. Covey was expected to to work in his family hotel business, but that wasn't the path for him. He wanted to make a different contribution—to be a teacher, to dedicate his life to unleashing human potential. "Every human being is precious," he wrote, "endowed with enormous, almost infinite potential and capacity."

To that end he studied at Harvard graduate school, became a university professor, and then widened his circle of influence as a consultant to business and government leaders. With the 1989 publication of *The 7 Habits of Highly Effective People*, considered by many the most influential book of our time, Dr. Covey had—and continues to have—worldwide impact. This book and his others can be found in home and office libraries literally around the globe.

Not only his teaching but his life reminds us of the power of enduring principles. He was not interested in riding fads or pandering for publicity. His passion was to articulate and teach the unchanging, immutable, and ageless truths of life—truths that apply equally well to professional success and to deep personal satisfaction. He also lived by those truths, as countless friends, family members, and students of Dr. Covey will attest.

Arranged under the decisive principles of life—such as integrity, life balance, vision, and love—the stories and quotations in this book teach those principles in accessible, gemlike form.

Although Dr. Covey has passed from us, we will always have the benefit of his timeless teachings—that truth is truth and is self-evident, that you can't live without principle and expect the universe to accommodate you, and that your life is a precious one that you can waste in mediocrity or invest in greatness.

—The Covey Family

NOTE TO READERS

This collection has been compiled from various books and articles. Each quotation is followed by a superscript number that corresponds to a reference list at the end of the book.

THE
PRINCIPLE
OF
ACCOUNTABILITY

My seven-year-old son Stephen volunteered to take care of the yard.

"Look, Son," I said. "See how our neighbor's yard is green and clean? That's what we're after: green and clean. Now come look at our yard. See the mixed colors? That's not it; that's not green. Green and clean is what we want."

Two weeks, two words: green and clean.

It was Saturday. And he did nothing. Sunday . . . nothing. Monday . . . nothing. As I pulled out of the driveway on my way to work on Tuesday, I looked at the yellow, cluttered yard and the hot July sun on its way up.

This was not acceptable. I was upset and disillusioned by his performance.

I was ready to go back to "gofer" delegation. But what would happen to his internal commitment?

So I faked a smile. "Hi, Son. How's it going?"

"Fine!" he returned.

I bit my tongue and waited until after dinner. Then I said, "Son, let's do as we agreed. Let's walk around the yard together and you can show me how it's going in your stewardship."

As we started out the door, his chin began to quiver. Tears

3

welled up in his eyes, and by the time we got out to the middle of the yard, he was whimpering.

"It's so hard, Dad!"

What's so hard? I thought to myself. You haven't done a single thing! But I knew what was hard—self-management, self-supervision. So I said, "Is there anything I can do to help?"

"Would you, Dad?" he sniffed.

"What was our agreement?"

"You said you'd help me if you had time."

"I have time."

So he ran into the house and came back with two sacks. He handed me one. "Will you pick that stuff up?" He pointed to the garbage from Saturday night's barbecue. "It makes me sick!"

So I did. I did exactly what he asked me to do. And that was when he signed the agreement in his heart. It became his yard, his stewardship.

He only asked for help two or three more times that entire summer. He took care of that yard. He kept it greener and cleaner than it had ever been under my stewardship.⁷

⁊⁊

Accountability breeds response-ability.³

⁊⁊

All of us are interested in things outside of our steward-ship, and we should be, but the most important way to do anything about them is to magnify our own stewardship.[4]

◈

Holding people to the responsible course is not demeaning; it is affirming.[7]

◈

It is one thing to make a mistake, and quite another thing not to admit it. People will forgive mistakes, because mis-takes are usually of the mind, mistakes of judgment. But people will not easily forgive the mistakes of the heart, the ill intention, the bad motives, the prideful, justifying cov-erup of the first mistake.[7]

◈

Never use the word promise unless you are totally prepared to pay whatever the price is to keep it.[8]

◈

Nothing destroys trust faster than making and breaking a promise. Conversely, nothing builds trust more than keeping a promise.[8]

ॐ

Sheltering people from natural consequences teaches irresponsibility.[4]

ॐ

The cause of almost all relationship difficulties is rooted in conflicting or ambiguous expectations around roles and goals.[7]

ॐ

The principle of stewardship is the principle of focusing on your own responsibility, on your own assignment, whatever that might be. You so focus on your duty as to magnify it—that is, to do more than is normally expected, to make more out of it than existed before. For instance, as a husband you focus on your responsibility of being a noble example to your children and a kind, understanding companion to your wife.[4]

ॐ

To improve any situation, you must improve. To change your wife, you must change. To change the attitude of your husband, you must change your attitude. To win more freedom, you must be more responsible, must exercise more discipline.[4]

❧

To raise obedient children, you and I as parents must be more obedient to certain laws and principles.[4]

❧

To rebuild broken-down relationships, we must first of all study our own hearts to discover our own responsibilities, our own faults. It is easy to stand at the sidelines and pick at others' weaknesses. This process serves only to feed our own pride and to justify ourselves.[4]

❧

We are not our feelings. We are not our moods. We are not even our thoughts. . . . Self-awareness enables us to stand apart and examine even the way we "see" ourselves.[7]

❧

Without involvement, there is no commitment. Mark it down, asterisk it, circle it, underline it. No involvement, no commitment.[7]

THE
PRINCIPLE
OF
BALANCE

Imagine you were to come upon someone in the woods working feverishly to saw down a tree.

"What are you doing?" you ask.

"Can't you see?" comes the impatient reply. "I'm sawing down this tree."

"You look exhausted!" you exclaim. "How long have you been at it?"

"Over five hours," he returns, "and I'm beat! This is hard work."

"Well, why don't you take a break for a few minutes and sharpen the saw?" you inquire. "I'm sure it would go a lot faster."

"I don't have time to sharpen the saw," the man says emphatically. "I'm too busy sawing![7]

ℐℐ

Have you ever been too busy driving to stop for gas?[10]

ℐℐ

How many people on their deathbeds wish they'd spent more time at the office?[1]

⚮

Many people seem to think that success in one area can compensate for failure in other areas. But can it really? True effectiveness requires balance.[7]

⚮

The key is not to prioritize what's on your schedule, but to schedule your priorities.[7]

⚮

There's a time for the mind to rule and a time for the heart to rule.[20]

⚮

We must never become too busy sawing to take time to sharpen the saw.[3]

⚮

THE
PRINCIPLE
OF
CHOICE

Once when I was speaking on the subject of proactivity, a woman in the audience stood up in the middle of my presentation and started talking excitedly. She seemed so happy.

"You just can't imagine what's happened to me!" she exclaimed. "I'm a full-time nurse to the most miserable, ungrateful man you can possibly imagine. Nothing I do is good enough for him. He never expresses appreciation; he hardly even acknowledges me. He constantly harps at me and finds fault with everything I do. This man has made my life miserable, and I often take my frustration out on my family. The other nurses feel the same way. We almost pray for his demise.

"And for you to have the gall to stand up there and suggest that nothing can hurt me, that no one can hurt me without my consent, and that I have chosen my own emotional life of being miserable—well, there was just no way I could buy into that.

"But I kept thinking about it. I really went inside myself and began to ask, 'Do I have the power to choose my response?' When I finally realized that I do have that power, when I swallowed that bitter pill and realized that I had chosen to be miserable, I also realized that I could choose not to be miserable. At that moment I stood up. I felt as though I was being let out of prison. I wanted to yell to the whole world, 'I am free! I

am let out of prison! No longer am I going to be controlled by the treatment of some person.'" [7]

᳁

Each of us guards a gate of change that can be opened only from the inside.[7]

᳁

Every human being has four endowments—self-awareness, conscience, independent will, and creative imagination. These give us the ultimate human freedom: The power to choose, to respond, to change.[1]

᳁

Happiness, like unhappiness, is a proactive choice.[7]

᳁

Happiness—in part, at least—is the fruit of the desire and ability to sacrifice what we want now for what we want eventually.[7]

᳁

I am not a product of my circumstances. I am a product of my decisions.[21]

*

I teach people how to treat me by what I will allow.[21]

*

If I really want to improve my situation, I can work on the one thing over which I have control—myself.[7]

*

Between stimulus and response there is a space. In that space lies our freedom and power to choose our responses. In those choices lie our growth and our happiness.[8]

*

Independent will is our capacity to act. It gives us the power to transcend our paradigms, to swim upstream, to rewrite our scripts, to act based on principle rather than reacting based on emotion or circumstance.[1]

*

It's not what happens to us but our response to what happens to us that hurts us.[7]

❧

Light a match, and it can destroy a building or give light to a dark place—it's your choice.[21]

❧

On the rudder of a huge ship there is another mini-rudder called the trim-tab. By moving the trim-tab ever so slightly, the rudder is slowly moved, which eventually changes the whole direction of a huge ship. See yourself as a trim-tab. By making small changes, you begin to have reverberations on the organization and possibly change the whole culture.[3]

❧

One of my favorite stories is the Old Testament story of Joseph, who was sold into slavery in Egypt by his brothers at a young age.

Can you imagine how easy it would have been for him to languish in self-pity as a servant to Potiphar, to focus on the weaknesses of his brothers and his captors and on all he didn't have? But Joseph was proactive. And within a short period of time, he was running Potiphar's household. He was in charge of all that Potiphar had because the trust was so high.

Then the day came when Joseph was caught in a difficult situation and refused to compromise his integrity. As a result, he was unjustly imprisoned for thirteen years.

But again he was proactive. He worked within his circle of influence, and soon he was running the prison and eventually the entire nation of Egypt, second only to the Pharaoh.[7]

ঞ

Our behavior is a function of our decisions, not our conditions.[7]

ঞ

Our language is a very real indicator of the degree to which we see ourselves as proactive people. The language of reactive people absolves them of responsibility: "That's me. That's just the way I am. There's nothing I can do about it."[7]

ঞ

Our ultimate freedom is the right and power to decide how anybody or anything outside ourselves will affect us.[21]

ঞ

Past experiences often act like chains on the present and the future. Early impressions become lasting impressions. Habits work themselves into ruts. A mental attitude that "It can't be done" becomes a self-fulfilling prophecy.[4]

ৰ৶৹

Reactive people are often affected by their physical environment. If the weather is good, they feel good. If it isn't, it affects their attitude and their performance. Proactive people can carry their own weather with them. Whether it rains or shines makes no difference to them.[7]

ৰ৶৹

Reactive people tend to live out of old programs given to them by others. They tend to be firefighters, impulsively running to and fro.[21]

ৰ৶৹

Setbacks are inevitable; misery is a choice.[8]

ৰ৶৹

The ability to subordinate an impulse to a value is the essence of the proactive person.[7]

✑

When you get into victimism, you give your future away. I was training insurance general agents one time, and they were all complaining about the terrible training programs of the company. I said, "Well, why don't you change them?"

They said, "What do you mean?"

"Well, you're not happy with these training programs. You feel that they're just a big laser show and there's no sharing of best practices. Why don't you change them?"

"Well, that's not our role."

I said, "Look, you're not victims. You're the top general agents in the company. You can make any presentation you want to the top decision makers; and if you make that presentation wisely—in other words, argue their case better for them than they can before you argue yours—you'll become change agents."[12]

✑

The environment you fashion out of your thoughts, your beliefs, your ideals, and your philosophy is the only climate you will ever live in.[11]

✑

21

The reflection of the current social paradigm tells us we are largely determined by conditioning and circumstances.[7]

✌

There are certain crucial moments in any human endeavor which, if excellently used, become the determining moments of the future. Be strong in the hard moments.[4]

✌

There are three constants in life: Change, Choice, and Principles.[21]

✌

Until a person can say deeply and honestly, "I am what I am today because of the choices I made yesterday," that person cannot say, "I choose otherwise."[7]

✌

We are free to choose our actions, but we are not free to choose the consequences of those actions. Remember, if you pick up one end of the stick, you pick up the other.[7]

✌

You are not your habits. You can replace old patterns of self-defeating behavior with new patterns, new habits of effectiveness.[7]

ঐৎ

One time a student asked me, "Will you excuse me from class? I have to go on a tennis trip."

"You have to go, or you choose to go?" I asked.

"I really have to," he explained.

"What will happen if you don't?"

"Why, they'll kick me off the team."

"How would you like that consequence?"

"I wouldn't."

"In other words, you choose to go because you want the consequence of staying on the team. What will happen if you miss my class?"

"I don't know."

"Think hard. What do you think would be the natural consequence of not coming to class?"

"You wouldn't kick me out, would you?"

"That would be a social consequence. That would be artificial. If you don't participate on the tennis team, you don't play. That's natural. But if you don't come to class, what would be the natural consequence?"

"I guess I'll miss the learning."

"That's right. So you have to weigh that consequence

against the other consequence and make a choice. I know if it were me, I'd choose to go on the tennis trip. But never say you have to do anything."

"I choose to go on the tennis trip," he meekly replied.

"And miss my class?"[7]

⚬⚬⚬

THE
PRINCIPLE
OF
CONTRIBUTION

A relative of mine has worked for IBM his entire professional life. He has thrived through every transformation of a dynamic company, working hard to stay relevant in an industry that revolutionizes itself every few years. He is very good at his work, which he takes seriously. His clients like him a lot. Even more important, he enjoys a great family life. He is not ambitious in the sense of needing the signs of external success, like constant promotions or public acclaim, but he's making a difference.

To me, that's a great career. He gives the best he has to give, while earning the loyalty and trust of clients, co-workers, and his family.

Many people argue about ambition. Is it a good or a bad thing? I believe it depends on the object of the ambition. . . . If you're ambitious to make a real difference—a meaningful contribution—you will experience the deep satisfaction of a job well done and a life well lived. That is the kind of ambition I believe in.[2]

৵৹

Anyone who has really made a difference for good or ill possessed three common attributes: vision, discipline, and passion. Hitler had all three, but he lacked a fourth essential attribute—conscience. The result was destruction.[7]

⸎

Be a light, not a judge. Be a model, not a critic.[7]

⸎

Deep within each of us is an inner longing to live a life of greatness and contribution—to really matter, to really make a difference. We can consciously decide to leave behind a life of mediocrity and to live a life of greatness—at home, at work, and in the community.[8]

⸎

Effectiveness is no longer optional. The call and need of a new era is for greatness.[8]

⸎

Look at the weaknesses of others with compassion, not accusation. It's not what they're not doing or should be doing that's the issue. The issue is your own chosen response to the situation and what you should be doing.[7]

❧

Man is not lazy or indifferent by nature. His natural and spiritual endowments give him boundless energy and enthusiasm. Every day we see these qualities manifested in activities in which he discovers personal meaning and significance.[4]

❧

Most of us spend too much time on what is urgent and not enough time on what is important.[21]

❧

Primary greatness means character and contribution. Secondary greatness is prestige and wealth and position.[21]

❧

The best a man can be, he must be.[4]

❧

The enemy of the best is often the good.[7]

ॐ

The key to life is not accumulation. It's contribution.[21]

ॐ

The most significant work we'll do in our whole life, in our whole world, is done within the four walls of our home.[21]

ॐ

The world's culture in which we are enmeshed primarily embraces material and social goals and values, which are often inconsistent with self-fulfilling goals and values.[4]

ॐ

There are achievers and there are contributors. Many achievers also contribute, but mostly they are just preparing to contribute. See your life as the life of a contributor.[21]

ॐ

THE
PRINCIPLE
OF
COURAGE

There was an acquaintance of mine who was very frustrated because his boss was locked into what he felt was an unproductive leadership style.

"Why doesn't he do anything?" he asked me. "I've talked to him about it, he's aware of it, but he does nothing."

"Well, why don't you make an effective presentation?" I asked.

"I did," was the reply.

"How do you define 'effective'? Who do they send back to school when the salesman doesn't sell—the buyer? 'Effective' means it works. Did you create the change you wanted? Did you build the relationship in the process? What were the results of your presentation?"

"I told you, he didn't do anything. He wouldn't listen."

"Then make an effective presentation. You've got to empathize with his head. You've got to get into his frame of mind. You've got to make your point simply and visually and describe the alternative he is in favor of better than he can himself. That will take some homework. Are you willing to do that?"

"Why do I have to go through all that?" he asked.

"In other words, you want him to change his whole lead-

33

ership style and you're not willing to change your method of presentation?"

"I guess so," he replied.

"Well then," I said, "just smile about it and learn to live with it."

"I can't live with it," he said. "It compromises my integrity."

"Okay, then get to work on an effective presentation."

In the end, he wouldn't do it. The investment seemed too great.[7]

cho

Many people think in dichotomies, in either/or terms. They think if you're nice, you're not tough. But win-win thinking is nice . . . and tough.[7]

cho

The greatest risk is the risk of riskless living.[8]

cho

The only real way to strengthen a relationship that has been strained is on a one-to-one basis—to go to that person to make reconciliation, to talk the matter over, to apologize, to forgive, or whatever it might take.[21]

ℐ

Where we have no control over a problem, our responsibility is to change the bottom line on our face—to smile, to genuinely and peacefully accept the problem and learn to live with it, even though we don't like it. In this way, we do not empower the problem to control us.[7]

ℐ

THE
PRINCIPLE
OF
EFFECTIVENESS

Remember the story of a poor farmer who one day discovers in the nest of his pet goose a glittering golden egg? At first he thinks it must be some kind of trick. But as he starts to throw the egg aside, he has second thoughts and takes it in to be appraised. The egg is pure gold! The farmer can't believe his good fortune. He becomes even more incredulous the following day when the experience is repeated.

Day after day, he awakens to rush to the nest and find another golden egg. He becomes fabulously wealthy; it all seems too good to be true. But with his increasing wealth comes greed and impatience.

Unable to wait day after day for the golden eggs, the farmer decides he will kill the goose and get them all at once. But when he opens the goose, he finds it empty. There are no golden eggs—and now there is no way to get any more. The farmer has destroyed the goose that produced them.

I suggest that within this fable is a natural law, a principle—the basic definition of effectiveness. Most people see effectiveness from the golden egg paradigm: The more you produce, the more you do, the more effective you are. If you adopt a pattern of life that focuses on golden eggs and neglects the goose, you will soon be without the asset that produces golden eggs.

On the other hand, if you only take care of the goose with no aim toward the golden eggs, you soon won't have the wherewithal to feed yourself or the goose. Effectiveness lies in the balance.[7]

෫ඌ

Highly effective people share 7 Habits. Habit 1 says "You're the programmer" and Habit 2 says "Write the program"; then Habit 3 says "Run the program," "Live the program." Habit 7 is the paradigm of continuous improvement of the whole person; it stands for education, learning, and recommitment.[7]

෫ඌ

All the well-meaning advice in the world won't amount to a hill of beans if we're not even addressing the real problem.[7]

෫ඌ

Any time we think the problem is "out there," that very thought is the problem.[7]

෫ඌ

Effective people are not problem-minded; they're opportunity-minded. They feed opportunities and starve problems.[7]

∽

Habit is the intersection of knowledge (what to do), skill (how to do), and desire (want to do).[7]

∽

How much negative energy is typically expended when people try to solve problems or make decisions in an interdependent reality? How much time is spent in confessing other people's sins, politicking, rivalry, interpersonal conflict, protecting one's backside, masterminding, and second guessing? It's like trying to drive down the road with one foot on the gas and the other foot on the brake.[7]

∽

In all of life there are stages or processes of growth and development. We know and accept this fact in the area of physical things, but understanding it in emotional areas, in human relations, and even in the spiritual area is less common and more difficult.[4]

∽

Independent thinking alone is not suited to interdependent reality. Independent people who do not have the maturity to think and act interdependently may be good individual producers, but they won't be good leaders or team players. They're not coming from the paradigm of interdependence necessary to succeed in marriage, family, or organizational reality.[7]

❧

It is possible to be busy—very busy—without being very effective.[7]

❧

Live, love, laugh, leave a legacy.[6]

❧

People are working harder than ever, but because they lack clarity and vision, they aren't getting very far. They, in essence, are pushing a rope with all of their might.[8]

❧

People simply feel better about themselves when they're good at something.[8]

❧

Some people have character strength but they lack the competency to communicate, and that undoubtedly affects the quality of their relationships as well. [3]

❧

The main thing is to keep the main thing the main thing. [1]

❧

There is no quick fix to chronic problems. To solve these, we must apply natural processes. The only way we can reap the harvest in the fall is to plant in the spring and to water, weed, cultivate, and fertilize during the long summer. [3]

❧

There's no better way to inform and expand your mind on a regular basis than to get into the habit of reading good literature. [7]

❧

To maintain the balance between the golden egg (production) and the health and welfare of the goose (production

43

capability) is often a difficult judgment call. But I suggest it is the very essence of effectiveness.[7]

⁂

We live in a shortcut world. Can you imagine a farmer "cramming" in the fall to bring forth the harvest, as students have done, and still do, to pass examinations? Can you imagine a mile runner "pretending" speed and endurance, or a concert pianist "putting on the appearance" of skill and proficiency?[4]

⁂

When it comes to developing character strength, inner security, and unique talents and skills in a child, no institution can or ever will compare with the home's potential for positive influence.[21]

⁂

You can be a transition person—a change for the better between the past and the future. A negative tendency that's run through your family for generations can stop with you. And your own change can affect many, many lives downstream.[7]

THE
PRINCIPLE
OF
EMPATHY

Suppose you've been having trouble with your eyes and you decide to go to an optometrist for help. After briefly listening to your complaint, he takes off his glasses and hands them to you.

"Put these on," he says. "I've worn this pair of glasses for ten years now and they've really helped me. I have an extra pair at home; you can wear these."

So you put them on, but it only makes the problem worse.

"This is terrible!" you exclaim. "I can't see a thing!"

"Well, what's wrong?" he asks. "They work great for me. Try harder."

"I am trying," you insist. "Everything is a blur."

"Well, what's the matter with you? Think positively."

"Okay. I positively can't see a thing."

"Boy, you are ungrateful!" he chides. "And after all I've done to help you!"

What are the chances you'd go back to that optometrist the next time you need help? Not very good, I would imagine. You don't have much confidence in someone who doesn't diagnose before he or she prescribes.

But how often do we diagnose before we prescribe in communication?[7]

჻

As you care less about what people think of you, you will care more about what others think of themselves.[7]

჻

At some time in your life, you probably had someone believe in you when you didn't believe in yourself.[7]

჻

Being influenceable is the key to influencing others.[7]

჻

Don't be seduced by your own autobiography.[21]

჻

Empathic listening is listening with intent to understand. I mean seeking first to understand, to really understand. Empathic listening gets inside another person's frame of reference. You look out through it, you see the world the way they see the world, you understand their paradigm, you understand how they feel.[7]

∽

Empathy enlarges your own thinking. When your spouse or your co-worker or your friend really opens up to you and becomes transparent to you, he injects his views into yours. His truths now belong to you as well.[5]

∽

Empathy is not sympathy. Sympathy is a form of agreement. Empathy is not agreeing with someone; it is fully, deeply understanding that person, emotionally as well as intellectually.[7]

∽

Fear is a knot of the heart, and to untie these knots is a matter of sincere, genuine, honest, affirming relationship. It is not so much a matter of intellectual understanding at all![4]

∽

I have made it a regular practice to interview my children. The basic ground rule in this "interview" is that I only listen and try to understand. It is not a time for moralizing, preaching, teaching, or disciplining—there are other times for that—this is a time to merely listen and understand and empathize. Sometimes I want terribly to move in and advise, teach, judge, or sympathize, but I have inwardly determined that during these special visits I will only attempt to understand.[4]

♂

If all the air were suddenly sucked out of the room you're in right now, what would happen to you? You wouldn't care about anything except getting air. Survival would be your only motivation. But now that you have air, it doesn't motivate you. This is one of the greatest insights in the field of human motivations: Satisfied needs do not motivate. It's only the unsatisfied need that motivates. Next to physical survival, the greatest need of a human being is psychological survival—to be understood, to be affirmed, to be validated, to be appreciated. When you listen with empathy to another person, you give that person psychological air.[7]

♂

If I were to summarize in one sentence the single most important principle I have learned in the field of interpersonal relations, it would be this: Seek First to Understand, Then to Be Understood.[7]

ᴄᴊᴘ

If you prize the relationship you have with the other party in a negotiation, you'll listen to him actively, reflectively, and empathically. You won't listen superficially, just waiting for a chance to pounce. You'll show empathy because that's the kind of person you are, not just because it's in your best interest.[5]

ᴄᴊᴘ

Most arguments are not really disagreements but are rather little ego battles and misunderstandings.[4]

ᴄᴊᴘ

After I gave a presentation one day, a fellow faculty member told me about the poor relationship he had with his son. He said, "I do understand my son. I have lived my life, and I know exactly what kinds of problems my son is having. I can see the dangers and the pitfalls in the future if he does not take my advice."

I said to him, "Let me suggest to you that you try making the assumption that you do not understand your son and that you start from the beginning by listening to him and what he says, without any moral evaluation."

"I don't believe in it," he said, "but I will try it."

At eight o'clock in the evening his son stated, "Dad, I just don't think you understand me at all." Later this man told me he didn't want to go through all this, but he had promised himself he would listen. "All right, Son," he said. "I'll assume that I don't. Now tell me about yourself." They went on for three and a half hours.

He later told me with new gratitude that he never realized he did not know his son at all, that he had never really allowed his son to express himself, or to be. "My son and I have re-found each other. We are friends again." [4]

∽

Most people do not listen with the intent to understand; they listen with the intent to reply. They're either speaking or preparing to speak. They're filtering everything through their own paradigms, reading their autobiography into other people's lives. [7]

∽

One person's mission is another person's minutia. You may be working on a high-priority project when your six-year-old child interrupts with something that seems trivial to you, but it may be very important from his point of view. [7]

∽

Our conversations become collective monologues; we never really understand what's going on inside another human being.[7]

⁂

People are very tender, very sensitive inside. I don't believe age or experience makes much difference. Inside, even within the most toughened and calloused exteriors, are the tender feelings and emotions of the heart.[7]

⁂

People behave more on the basis of how they feel than how they think. Unless there are good feelings between people it is almost impossible to reason intelligently.[4]

⁂

People tend to become like you treat them or like you believe them to be.[21]

⁂

Rebellion is a knot of the heart, not of the mind.[7]

⁂

Seek first to understand, then to be understood.[7]

ॐ

The Golden Rule says to "Do unto others as you would have others do unto you." While on the surface that could mean to do for them what you would like to have done for you, I think the more essential meaning is to understand them deeply as individuals, the way you would want to be understood, and then to treat them in terms of that understanding.[7]

ॐ

The more deeply you understand other people, the more you will appreciate them, the more reverent you will feel about them. To touch the soul of another human being is to walk on holy ground.[7]

ॐ

When people are really hurting and you really listen with a pure desire to understand, you'll be amazed how fast they will open up. They want to open up, layer upon layer—it's like peeling an onion until you get to the soft inner core.[7]

ॐ

When the air is charged with emotions, an attempt to teach is often perceived as a form of judgment and rejection.[7]

◌◌

When we have problems in our interactions with other people, we're very aware of acute pain—it's often intense, and we want it to go away. That's when we try to treat the symptoms with quick fixes and techniques—the Band-Aids of the personality ethic. We don't understand that the acute pain is an outgrowth of the deeper, chronic problem.[7]

◌◌

When you have "no deal" as an option in your mind, you can honestly say, "I only want to go for win-win. I want to win, and I want you to win. I wouldn't want to get my way and have you not feel good about it, because downstream your bad feelings would eventually surface. On the other hand, I don't think you would feel good if you got your way at my expense. So let's work for a win-win. Let's really hammer it out. And if we can't find it, then let's agree that we won't make a deal at all. It would be better not to deal than to live with a decision that wasn't right for us both. Then maybe another time we might be able to get together."[7]

◌◌

Words are like eggs dropped from great heights. You could no more call them back than ignore the mess they left when they fell.[21]

❧

You can't think efficiency with people. You think effectiveness with people and efficiency with things.[7]

❧

A father once told me, "I can't understand my kid. He just won't listen to me at all."

"Let me restate what you just said," I replied. "You don't understand your son because he won't listen to you?"

"That's right," he replied.

"Let me try again," I said. "You don't understand your son because he won't listen to you?"

"That's what I said," he impatiently replied.

"I thought that to understand another person, you needed to listen to him," I suggested.

"Oh!" he said. There was a long pause. "Oh!" he said again, as the light began to dawn.[7]

❧

THE
PRINCIPLE
OF
INTEGRITY

Once, as I got into a cab outside a Canadian hotel, the bell-man told the driver to "take Dr. Covey to the airport." The driver assumed I was a physician and began to talk about his medical problems. I tried to explain that I wasn't that kind of doctor, but his English was limited and he didn't understand me. So I just listened.

He told me about his aches and pains and his double vision. The more he talked, the more I was convinced that his problems were due to a bad conscience. He complained about having to lie and cheat his way through the system to get fares. "I'm not gonna follow the rules . . . I know how to get those fares." Then his expression sobered. "But if the policemen find me, I will get in trouble. I will lose my license. What do you think, Doctor?"

I said to him, "Don't you think that the main source of all these tensions and pressures is that you're not being true to your conscience? You inwardly know what you should do."

"But I can't make a living that way!"

I talked to him about the peace of mind and wisdom that comes from living true to your conscience. "Don't cheat. Don't lie. Don't steal. Treat people with respect."

"You really think it would help?"

"I know it would."

As he dropped me off, he refused my tip. He just embraced me. "I'm gonna do that. I already feel better." [2]

❧

"Inside-Out" means to start first with self; even more fundamentally, to start with the most inside part of self—with your paradigms, your character, and your motives. Any time we think the problem is "out there," that thought is the problem. We empower what's out there to control us. The change paradigm is "outside-in"—what's out there has to change before we can change. [7]

❧

A life of pretense is a tortuous task. [4]

❧

Attending church does not necessarily mean living the principles taught in those meetings. You can be active in a church but inactive in its gospel. [7]

❧

Churchgoing is not synonymous with personal spirituality. There are some people who get so busy in church worship and projects that they become insensitive to the pressing human needs that surround them, contradicting the very precepts they profess to believe deeply.[7]

∂∫

Don't argue for other people's weaknesses. Don't argue for your own. When you make a mistake, admit it, correct it, and learn from it—immediately.[7]

∂∫

From the time of birth a person belongs to one institution of society after another. Each one values or judges its members. These judgments accumulate and, taken together, tell or label or define just who the person is.[4]

∂∫

Frustration is a function of our expectations, and our expectations are often a reflection of the social mirror rather than our own values and priorities.[7]

∂∫

Honesty is telling the truth—in other words, conforming our words to reality. Integrity is conforming reality to our words—in other words, keeping promises and fulfilling expectations. This requires an integrated character, a oneness, primarily with self but also with life.[7]

❦

Humility is the greatest of all virtues because out of it come all the other virtues.[21]

❦

In becoming all things to all people, one eventually becomes nothing to everybody—particularly to oneself.[3]

❦

In developing our own self-awareness many of us discover ineffective scripts, deeply embedded habits that are totally unworthy of us, totally incongruent with the things we really value in life.[7]

❦

In the last analysis, what we are communicates far more eloquently than anything we say or do.[7]

❧

Loyalty must not be a higher value than integrity; in fact, real integrity is loyalty. You want your doctor to tell you the truth even if you don't want to hear it.[8]

❧

Make a little promise to yourself and keep it; then a little bigger one, then a bigger one. Eventually, your sense of honor will become greater than your moods; and when that happens, you'll discover the true source of power—moral authority.[8]

❧

Many believe that the only things we need for success are talent, energy, and personality. But history has taught us that, over the long haul, who we are is more important than who we appear to be.[8]

❧

Many people with secondary greatness—that is, social recognition for their talents—lack primary greatness or goodness in their character. Sooner or later, you'll see this in every long-term relationship they have, whether it is with a business associate, a spouse, a friend, or a teenage child going through an identity crisis. It is character that communicates most eloquently.[7]

❦

No wonder many feel anxious and fearful, and live to pretend, to impress. Their lives are buffeted by outside changing forces rather than being anchored by the changeless intrinsic value within.[4]

❦

One of the most important ways to manifest integrity is to be loyal to those who are not present. In doing so, we build the trust of those who are present. When you defend those who are absent, you retain the trust of those present.[7]

❦

Our character is basically a composite of our habits. Because they are consistent, often unconscious patterns, they constantly, daily, express our character.

People can't live with change if there's not a changeless core inside them. The key to the ability to change is a changeless sense of who you are, what you are about, and what you value.[7]

⤥

Principled people are not extremists—they do not make everything all or nothing. They do not divide everything into good or bad, either/or. They think in terms of continuums, priorities, hierarchies.[3]

⤥

The more a person cares about what other people think, the less he can afford to care about what other people think because he's too vulnerable to it.[3]

⤥

The roots of the problems we face in the world, in our national lives, and in our family and personal lives are spiritual. Like the leaves on a tree, the symptom manifestations of these problems are social, economic, and political. But the roots are moral and spiritual. And they lie first within each individual and then within the family.[4]

⤥

The unfulfilled person often prefers to sit back and watch others live. Playing one imaginary role after another, he soon loses knowledge of his own role and experiences himself only as others want him to be.[4]

✑

Virtue is lost a little at a time, by degrees.[4]

✑

We do not have a successful public victory—that is, an accomplished worthy task—unless we have a successful private victory.[4]

✑

We hear a lot about identity theft when someone takes your wallet and pretends to be you. But the more serious identity theft is to get swallowed up in other people's definition of you.[5]

✑

When we borrow our strength from the label on our shirt, sweater, shoes, or dress; from our association with a club; from our position of influence, power, and prestige; from our car, beautiful house, or other status symbols and trappings; or from our good looks, stylish clothing, fashionable appearance, clever tongue, or degrees and credentials, we do so in order to compensate for being impoverished and hollow inside. But by doing so, we reinforce our dependency on these symbols, on living by appearances, on extrinsic values, and we build weakness within.[4]

*

Wisdom is the child of integrity—being integrated around principles. And integrity is the child of humility and courage. In fact, you could say that humility is the mother of all virtues because humility acknowledges that there are natural laws or principles that govern the universe. They are in charge. Pride teaches us that we are in charge. Humility teaches us to understand and live by principles, because they ultimately govern the consequences of our actions. If humility is the mother, courage is the father of wisdom. Because to truly live by these principles when they are contrary to social mores, norms, and values takes enormous courage.[8]

*

You can't talk your way out of a problem you behaved your way into.[7]

ৡৡ

You have to decide what your highest priorities are and have the courage—pleasantly, smilingly, unapologetically—to say "no" to other things. And the way you do that is by having a bigger "yes" burning inside.[7]

ৡৡ

Your problems begin first in your own heart.[4]

ৡৡ

THE
PRINCIPLE
OF
LEADERSHIP

I had a visit with the top executives of a large organization, and I asked them to show me their corporate mission statement. It read something like "Maximize value for the shareholders."

I asked them, "Is everyone around here inspired by that?"

They smiled and said, "We have another statement that we post on the walls. But this is the one we in leadership live by."

So I said, "Why don't I tell you what your corporate culture is like. You're split apart. If your industry is unionized, you're plagued with labor disputes. You're hovering, checking up, and carrot-and-sticking your employees to do their jobs. There's an enormous amount of negative energy spent in interpersonal conflict, interdepartmental rivalries, hidden agendas, and political games."

Amazed at my fortune-telling skills, they asked, "How could you know so much? How could you describe us so accurately?"

I said, "I don't have to know much about your industry or you. All I have to know about is human nature."[8]

❦

Always treat your employees exactly as you want them to treat your best customers.[7]

❦

Are leaders born or made? This is a false dichotomy—leaders are neither born nor made. Leaders choose to be leaders.[8]

❦

Cultural moral authority always develops slower than institutionalized or visionary moral authority.[8]

❦

Effective leadership is putting first things first. Effective management is discipline, carrying it out.[7]

❦

I don't define leadership as becoming the CEO. A CEO is no more likely to be a leader than anyone else. I am talking about leading your own life, being a leader among your friends, being a leader in your own family.[5]

❦

If you put good people in bad systems, you get bad results. You have to water the flowers you want to grow.[7]

⁋

In the Industrial Age, leadership was a position. In the Knowledge Age, leadership is a choice.[13]

⁋

It is easy for a task-oriented leader just to keep pushing things along and unintentionally to ignore the feelings that are aroused and the relationships that develop in the process.

Leaders are often tossed and turned by every wind of new leadership "doctrine." Should they be more democratic or more autocratic in action? Firmer or more permissive? Tell more or ask more? What are the best techniques for getting things done through people? These questions are important and must be considered, but they are secondary questions. The primary question is: How much do you really care?[4]

⁋

Leaders who take an interest in people merely because they should will be both wrong and unsuccessful. They will be wrong because regard for people is an end in itself. They will be unsuccessful because they will be found out.

❧

Leadership is a choice that lies in the space between stimulus and response.[8]

❧

Leadership is the highest of the arts, simply because it enables all the other arts and professions to work.[8]

❧

Management works in the system; leadership works on the system[1].

❧

Only when people are sincerely and meaningfully involved are they willing to commit the best that is within them.[4]

❧

In this topsy-turvy world . . . we confuse efficiency with effectiveness, expediency with priority, imitation with innovation, cosmetics with character, or pretense with competence.[3]

ℐℛ

Some leaders are into "mushroom management": "Keep people in the dark, pile lots of manure on them, and, when they are fully ripe, cut off their heads and can them."[3]

ℐℛ

The problem of leadership today is that managers are still applying the Industrial Age control model to knowledge workers. They fail to tap into the highest motivations, talents, and genius of their people.[8]

ℐℛ

The psychology behind our accounting system is stupid. People are an expense and things are an investment, when in truth it's the other way around.[14]

ℐℛ

Leadership is communicating to people their worth and potential so clearly that they come to see it in themselves.[9]

ℐℛ

Verbal, logical, and analytical work is generally left-brain work; if it's more intuitive, emotional, or creative work, it would be right-brain work. I suggest this: Manage from the left, lead from the right.[3]

ঞ

When parents see their children's problems as opportunities to build the relationship instead of as negative, burdensome irritations, it totally changes the nature of parent-child interaction. When a child comes to them with a problem, instead of thinking, "Oh, no! Not another problem!" their paradigm is, "Here is a great opportunity for me to really help my child and to invest in our relationship."[7]

ঞ

While many of us might give lip service to the importance of parenthood responsibility, often we will give our prime energy, enthusiasm, time, and loyalty to our professions. We will approach our work with careful planning, using the best systems, keeping careful records, spending time to analyze problems; but with the character development of our own children we might go on day in and day out without any real analysis or planning or record keeping, without any intelligent system. [4]

⚮

You can buy a person's hand, but you can't buy his heart. His heart is where his enthusiasm, his loyalty is. You can buy his back, but you can't buy his brain. That's where his creativity is, his ingenuity, his resourcefulness.[7]

⚮

You can't change the fruit without changing the root.[7]

⚮

You can quickly grasp the important difference between leadership and management if you envision a group of producers cutting their way through the jungle with machetes. They're the producers, the problem solvers. They're cutting through the undergrowth, clearing it out.

The managers are behind them, sharpening their machetes, writing policy and procedure manuals, holding muscle-development programs, bringing in improved technologies, and setting up working schedules and compensation programs for machete wielders.

The leader is the one who climbs the tallest tree, surveys the entire situation, and yells, "Wrong jungle!" But how do the busy, efficient producers and managers often respond? "Shut up! We're making progress."[7]

❧

THE
PRINCIPLE
OF
LEARNING

Twice a year students from the Indian Institute of Manage-ment at Ahmedabad go on a pilgrimage into the countryside for eight to ten days. On this shodhyatra, or "foot trek," the stu-dent pilgrims are looking for 3rd Alternatives—the odd idea, the strange or new creation born of necessity in the remote vil-lages of India. The shodhyatris are fascinated by the smallest positive deviation. If they find some unusual practice or device invented by a farmer or shop worker, they bring it back to be shared through the Honey Bee Network, a national organiza-tion dedicated to leveraging the new knowledge. . . .

The shodhyatris dutifully record herbal remedies, odd uses of small motors (e.g., an old Sony Walkman used to power a fan), and even local recipes for curry. They also encounter small miracles, like a child who can recite the names and uses of more than three hundred local plants. Often they find truly innova-tive ideas that can transform the lives of the poor. One suc-cessful find was Mansukh Prajapati's "Mitti Cool" refrigerator made from an ingenious rectangular clay pot and requiring no electricity; thousands of them are in use. He has also invented a plow driven by a motorcycle and a nonstick clay pan that reportedly works as well as a Teflon pan but costs only a dollar.

The inventor of a device for climbing coconut trees is now selling his climber internationally. An herbal cream for eczema that came out of a farm village has become popular around the world. Another man invented an amphibious bicycle so he could cross the river to see his girlfriend. "I couldn't wait for the boat," he says. "I had to meet my love. My desperation made me an innovator. Even love needs help from technology."[5]

☙

The proactive approach to a mistake is to acknowledge it instantly, correct it, and learn from it. This literally turns a failure into a success.[7]

☙

Admission of ignorance is often the first step in our education.[7]

☙

Almost every significant breakthrough in the field of scientific endeavor is first a break with tradition, with old ways of thinking, with old paradigms.[7]

☙

Educate and obey your conscience. Educate your conscience by studying literature that inspires you the most. Then obey it. Little by little, as you obey it, you will get more education. More and more light will come.[21]

~

Educating the heart is the critical complement to educating the mind.[1]

~

I believe in a system of some kind for self-education. It doesn't have to be formal classes or courses. It may be an informal discussion group or a well-conceived reading program. But without some system or external discipline, most adults tend to give up after a good start on something and fall back to old ways.[4]

~

If we do not teach our children, society will. And they—and we—will live with the results.[6]

~

If you organize your family life to spend even ten or fifteen minutes a morning reading something that connects you with timeless principles, it's almost guaranteed that you will make better choices during the day—in the family, on the job, in every dimension of life. Your thoughts will be higher. Your interactions will be more satisfying. You will have a greater perspective. You will increase that space between what happens to you and your response to it. You will be more connected to what really matters most.[6]

The main value of education is not financial or occupational, but it is personal and spiritual and character-building. You can become a better husband and father, wife and mother, and citizen. You learn to think analytically and creatively. You learn to write and communicate clearly and persuasively. You learn how to read with discrimination. You develop a way of thinking about life and problems. Your basic knowledge is deepened and expanded, your horizons lifted. Your ability to sympathize and appreciate is increased. In every way you can become a fuller and more integrated, more capable, wiser human being.[4]

To know and not to do is really not to know.[7]

๛

True knowledge is a state of being.[4]

๛

When the president of the United States asked me what was needed to improve education in our country, I responded, "Partnerships between schools and parents in educating the whole child, which includes developing both the character strength and the competencies required to really succeed in the twenty-first century."[15]

๛

THE
PRINCIPLE
OF
LOVE

A man cornered me once and confided to me, "My wife and I just don't have the same feelings for each other we used to have. I guess I just don't love her anymore and she doesn't love me. What can I do?"

"The feeling isn't there anymore?" I asked.

"That's right," he affirmed. "And we have three children we're really concerned about. What do you suggest?"

"Love her," I replied.

"I told you, the feeling just isn't there anymore."

"Love her."

"You don't understand. The feeling of love just isn't there."

"Then love her. If the feeling isn't there, that's a good reason to love her."

"But how do you love when you don't love?"

"My friend, love is a verb. Love—the feeling—is a fruit of love, the verb. So love her. Serve her. Sacrifice. Listen to her. Empathize. Appreciate. Affirm her. Are you willing to do that?"[7]

꧁꧂

How you treat the one reveals how you regard the many, because everyone is ultimately a one.[7]

✤

— I have a friend whose son developed an avid interest in baseball. My friend wasn't interested in baseball at all. But one summer, he took his son to see every major league team play one game. The trip took over six weeks and cost a great deal of money, but it became a powerful bonding experience in their relationship. My friend was asked on his return, "Do you like baseball that much?" "No," he replied, "but I like my son that much."[7]

✤

If I make deposits into an Emotional Bank Account with you through courtesy, kindness, honesty, and keeping my commitments to you, I build up a reserve. Your trust in me becomes higher, and I can call upon that trust many times if I need to. I can even make mistakes, and that trust level, that emotional reserve, will compensate for it. My communication may not be clear, but you'll get my meaning anyway. You won't make me "an offender for a word." When the trust account is high, communication is easy, instant, and effective.[7]

❧

If parents obey the laws of love, they encourage obedience to the laws of life.

If you want to have a more pleasant, cooperative teenager, be a more understanding, empathic, consistent, loving parent.[7]

❧

In relationships, the little things are the big things.[7]

❧

The ambitious individual is deeply concerned with his own things. He even regards his children as possessions and often attempts to wrest from them the kind of behavior that will win him more popularity and esteem in the eyes of others. This kind of possessive love is destructive.[4]

❧

The laws of love essentially amount to accepting people as they are, listening to them with understanding, respecting their feelings, and patiently and caringly building relationships.[4]

ॐ

Thomas Wolfe was wrong: You can go home again—if your home is a treasured relationship, a precious companionship.[7]

ॐ

THE
PRINCIPLE
OF
POTENTIAL

In the summer of 1988, Yellowstone National Park caught fire. At first no one worried; forest fires in Yellowstone are common and usually burn themselves out. But this one was different. Drought, wind, and excess fuel in the form of old trees and undergrowth combined to create a perfect firestorm. By summer's end more than a million acres had burned, and it seemed that Yellowstone—that jewel of a national park—had been destroyed forever.

But it wasn't so. Within a year, baby green pines carpeted the blackened landscape, and today—only a couple of decades later—fresh new forests have taken over. It turns out that only the heat of fire can stimulate the famous lodgepole pines of Yellowstone to re-seed themselves. As part of the natural order of things, the fire did not damage the park; it renewed the park.

The twenty-first-century economy is giving everyone a wild ride. It seems that turbulent times are here to stay. The seismic shift to a Knowledge Economy has so disoriented so many people that they have a hard time getting their footing. Some see only disaster, as if—like the Yellowstone fire—the future is turning to ashes. They see only millions of jobs gone up in smoke, whole industries laid waste, an economic landscape barren and scarce.

To others, the landscape has never been greener. The vola-tile, burned-over economy of the new century provides oppor-tunities no one ever dreamed of in industries that didn't even exist a few years ago. What seems to some a disaster holds the seeds of renewal for others. Have the problems of the world gone away? Does the world still cry out for energetic, intelligent people to do its work? Of course it does.[2]

☙

I am more than my grievances, my position, my ideology, my team, my company, or my party. I am not a victim of the past. I am a whole person, a unique individual, capable of shaping my own destiny.[5]

☙

I am personally convinced that one person can be a change catalyst, a "transformer" in any situation, any organization. Such an individual is yeast that can leaven an entire loaf. It requires vision, initiative, patience, respect, persistence, courage, and faith to be a transforming leader.[3]

☙

I frequently ask large audiences, "How many agree that the vast majority of the workforce in your organization possesses far more talent, intelligence, capability, and creativity than their present jobs require or even allow?" The overwhelming majority of the people raise their hands.[8]

✋

Imagine the personal and organizational cost of failing to fully engage the passion, talent, and intelligence of the workforce. It is far greater than all taxes, interest charges, and labor costs put together![8]

✋

Our most important financial asset is our own capacity to earn.[7]

✋

The 8th Habit is to find your voice and inspire others to find theirs.[8]

✋

Everyone chooses one of two roads in life—the old and the young, the rich and the poor, men and women alike. One is the broad, well-traveled road to mediocrity, the other the road to greatness and meaning.[8]

❧

Your voice lies at the nexus of talent, passion, need, and conscience. When you engage in work that taps your talent and fuels your passion—that rises out of a great need in the world that you feel drawn by conscience to meet—therein lies your voice, your calling, your soul's code.[8]

❧

We are self-aware. This awareness means that we can stand mentally outside of ourselves and evaluate our beliefs and our actions. We can think about what we think.[5]

❧

THE
PRINCIPLE
OF
SELF-DISCIPLINE

In the gym one day, I was working out with a friend of mine who has a PhD in exercise physiology. He was focusing on building strength. He asked me to "spot" him while he did some bench presses and told me at a certain point he'd ask me to take the weight. "But don't take it until I tell you," he said firmly.

So I watched and waited and prepared to take the weight. The weight went up and down, up and down. And I could see it begin to get harder. But he kept going. He would start to push it up and I'd think, "There's no way he's going to make it." But he'd make it. Then he'd slowly bring it back down and start back up again. Up and down, up and down.

As I looked at his face, straining with the effort, his blood vessels practically jumping out of his skin, I thought, "This is going to fall and collapse his chest. Maybe I should take the weight. Maybe he's lost control and he doesn't even know what he's doing." But he'd get it safely down. Then he'd start back up again. I couldn't believe it.

When he finally told me to take the weight, I said, "Why did you wait so long?"

"Almost all the benefit of the exercise comes at the very end, Stephen," he replied. "I'm trying to build strength. And that

101

doesn't happen until the muscle fiber ruptures and the nerve fiber registers the pain. Then nature overcompensates and, within forty-eight hours, the fiber is made stronger."

Now, the same principle works with emotional muscles as well, such as patience. When you exercise your patience beyond your past limits, the emotional fiber is broken, nature overcompensates, and next time the fiber is stronger.[7]

෨෨

Discipline derives from disciple—disciple to a philosophy, disciple to a set of principles, disciple to a set of values, disciple to an overriding purpose, to a superordinate goal or a person who represents that goal.[7]

෨෨

I make an effort every morning to win what I call the "private victory." I work out on a stationary bike while I am studying the Scriptures for at least thirty minutes. Then I swim in a pool vigorously for fifteen minutes, then I do yoga in a shallow part of the pool for fifteen minutes. Then I pray with a listening spirit, listening primarily to my conscience while I visualize the rest of my entire day, including important professional activities and key relationships with my loved ones, working associates, and clients. I see myself living by correct principles and accomplishing worthy purposes.[16]

✑

Listen to your conscience regarding something that you simply know you should do, then start small on it—make a promise and keep it. Then move forward and make a little larger promise and keep it. Eventually you'll discover that your sense of honor will become greater than your moods, and that will give you a level of confidence and excitement that you can move on to other areas where you feel you need to make improvements or give service.[16]

✑

Most people equate discipline with an absence of freedom. In fact, the opposite is true; only the disciplined are truly free. The undisciplined are slaves to moods, appetites, and passions.[8]

✑

Most people say their main fault is a lack of discipline. On deeper thought, I believe that is not the case. The basic problem is that their priorities have not become deeply planted in their hearts and minds.[7]

✑

Organizing on a weekly basis provides much greater balance and context than daily planning. Most people think in terms of weeks. There seems to be implicit cultural recognition of the week as a single, complete unit of time. Business, education, and many other facets of society operate within the framework of the week, designating certain days for focused investment and others for relaxation or inspiration.[7]

⌘

Private Victory precedes Public Victory. Self-mastery and self-discipline are the foundation of good relationships with others.[7]

⌘

Whip those procrastinating, undisciplined tendencies, those inclinations toward weakness. Do it in private—and I am telling you, you will sweat it out; it is not an easy thing—it is a most difficult thing—but take the time to do it, and watch the gradual serenity and power that will come into your life.[4]

⌘

Years ago we were all transfixed by the lunar voyages. Superlatives such as "fantastic" and "incredible" are inadequate to describe those eventful days.

Where was the most power and energy expended on those heavenly journeys? Going a quarter of a million miles to the moon? Returning to the earth? Orbiting the moon? Lift-off from the moon?

No, not these—not even all these together. Rather, it was on the lift-off from the earth. More energy was spent in the first few minutes of lift-off, in the first few miles of travel, than was used in half a million miles for several days. Habits also have a tremendous gravity pull.

Breaking deeply embedded habitual tendencies, such as procrastination, impatience, criticalness, or living in excesses or selfishness, involves more than a little willpower and a few minor changes in our lives.[4]

THE
PRINCIPLE
OF
SYNERGY

I belong to a world leadership group seeking to build a better relationship between the West and the Islamic community. It includes a former U.S. secretary of state, prominent imams and rabbis, global business leaders, and experts on conflict resolution. At our first meeting, it became obvious that everyone had an agenda. It was all rather formal and cool, and you could just feel the tension. That was on a Sunday.

I asked permission from the group to teach them one principle before we went any further, and they graciously agreed. So I taught them [the principle of synergy].

By Tuesday night the whole atmosphere had changed. The private agendas had been shelved. We had arrived at an exciting resolution that we had never anticipated. The people in the room were filled with respect and love for one another— you could see it, and you could feel it. The former secretary of state whispered to me, "I've never seen anything so powerful. What you've done here could totally revolutionize international diplomacy."[5]

Certainly we need law or else society will deteriorate. It provides survival, but it doesn't create synergy. At best it results in compromise.[7]

∽

Conflict is a sign of life. Conflicts usually arise when people are actually thinking about their work. When I talk about the "gift of conflict," people look sideways at me, but what I mean is that thoughtful people will always differ from each other—and that if they care enough to express their differences with passion, that's an offering that ought to be accepted eagerly.[5]

∽

Every child is a 3rd Alternative, a distinctive human being endowed with capabilities that have never existed before and will never be duplicated. Those capabilities cannot be predicted by adding up the capabilities of the parents. The particular combination of human endowments in that child is unique in the universe, and the creative potential of the child is exponentially great.[5]

∽

How does someone create a win-win situation in business? What happens when one side benefits more? When one side benefits more than the other, that's a win-lose situation. To the winner it might look like success for a while, but in the long run it breeds resentment and distrust. You get to win-win simply by asking, "How could we both win in this situation?" What you're looking for is a 3rd Alternative that's superior to anything you could create alone.[17]

ℐℐ

If two people have the same opinion, one is unnecessary.[7]

ℐℐ

Insecure people think that all reality should be amenable to their paradigms. They have a high need to clone others, to mold them over into their own thinking. They don't realize that the very strength of the relationship is in having another point of view. Sameness is not oneness; uniformity is not unity.[7]

ℐℐ

Involve people in the problem, immerse them in it, so that they soak it in and feel it is their problem and they tend to become an important part of the solution.[7]

ℐℐ

Is it logical that two people can disagree and that both can be right? It's not logical: it's psychological. And it's very real.[7]

ℐℐℐ

It's exciting when you truly hear out divergent views and you start to see how to bring them together for a solution nobody ever thought of before. Of course, the barriers are defensiveness, territoriality, the not-invented-here syndrome.[17]

ℐℐℐ

Many people have not really experienced even a moderate degree of synergy in their family life or in other interactions. They've been trained and scripted into defensive and protective communications or into believing that life or other people can't be trusted.[7]

ℐℐℐ

Most entrepreneurs have a tendency toward independence. They like to do things on their own. But if you go to the Entrepreneur of the Year meetings every year, you'll see that those who win consistently win as a team.[14]

◦◦◦

Most meetings are a waste of time, because they are so ill-prepared and there's so little opportunity for true synergy in producing better solutions.[16]

◦◦◦

Most negotiators are trying to get their way. Through rounds of haggling, they usually arrive at a compromise, in which both sides concede something to get an agreement. By contrast, a 3rd Alternative requires no concessions at all because it's truly a better deal for everyone. You get to it not by haggling but by asking, "Would you be willing to go for a 3rd Alternative that is better than what either of us has in mind?"[17]

◦◦◦

Public Victory does not mean victory over other people. It means success in effective interaction that brings mutually beneficial results to everyone involved. Public Victory means working together, communicating together, making things happen together that even the same people couldn't make happen by working independently.[7]

ᴕᴘ

True innovation depends on synergy, and synergy requires diversity. Two people who see things in exactly the same way cannot synergize. In their case, one plus one equals two. But two people who see things differently can synergize, and for them one plus one can equal three or ten or a thousand.[5]

ᴕᴘ

Synergy is everywhere in nature. If you plant two plants close together, the roots commingle and improve the quality of the soil so that both plants will grow better than if they were separated. If you put two pieces of wood together, they will hold much more than the total of the weight held by each separately. The whole is greater than the sum of its parts. One plus one equals three or more.[7]

ᴕᴘ

Synergy is not the same as compromise. In a compromise, one plus one equals one and a half at best.[5]

ᴕᴘ

The first step in the synergy process is to ask this question: "Are you willing to go for a solution that is better than either one of us has in mind?"[5]

⸎

The transactional approach to conflict is all about "me": "How do I get what I want with the least possible damage?" The transformational approach to conflict is all about "we": "How do we create something amazing together?"[5]

⸎

Valuing the differences is the essence of synergy—the mental, the emotional, the psychological differences between people. And the key to valuing those differences is to realize that all people see the world, not as it is, but as they are.[7]

⸎

When people can't compromise, that can be a good thing—because the way might be open to a 3rd Alternative. With a compromise we all lose something; with a 3rd Alternative, we all win.[18]

⸎

THE
PRINCIPLE
OF
TRUST

I know of a restaurant that served a fantastic clam chowder and was packed with customers every day at lunchtime. Then the business was sold, and the new owner focused on golden eggs—he decided to water down the chowder.

For about a month, with costs down and revenues constant, profits zoomed. But little by little, the customers began to disappear. Trust was gone, and business dwindled to almost nothing. The new owner tried desperately to reclaim it, but he had neglected the customers, violated their trust, and lost the asset of customer loyalty. There was no more goose to produce the golden egg.[7]

ℐℓ

If you want to be trusted, be trustworthy.[7]

ℐℓ

To retain the trust of those who are present, be loyal to those who are absent.[7]

ℐℓ

People instinctively trust those whose personality is founded upon correct principles.[3]

⸿

There are people we trust absolutely because we know their character. Whether they're eloquent or not, whether they have the human relations techniques or not, we trust them, and we work successfully with them.[7]

⸿

Trust is the glue of life. It's the most essential ingredient in effective communication. It's the foundational principle that holds all relationships together.[1]

⸿

Trust is the highest form of human motivation.[7]

⸿

We all know what a financial bank account is. We make deposits into it and build up a reserve from which we can make withdrawals when we need to. An Emotional Bank Account is a metaphor that describes the amount of trust that's been built up in a relationship. It's the feeling of safeness you have with another human being. If I make deposits into an Emotional Bank Account with you through courtesy, kindness, honesty, and keeping my commitments to you, I build up a reserve.[7]

✣

When there is high trust, communication is easy, effortless, instantaneous. If you make a mistake, it hardly matters. People know you.[8]

✣

THE
PRINCIPLE
OF
TRUTH

I remember a mini-paradigm shift I experienced one Sunday morning on a subway in New York. People were sitting quietly—some reading newspapers, some lost in thought, some resting with their eyes closed. It was a calm, peaceful scene.

Then suddenly, a man and his children entered the subway car. The children were so loud and rambunctious that instantly the whole climate changed.

The man sat down next to me and closed his eyes, apparently oblivious to the situation. The children were yelling back and forth, throwing things, even grabbing people's papers. It was very disturbing. And yet, the man sitting next to me did nothing.

It was difficult not to feel irritated. I could not believe that he could be so insensitive to let his children run wild like that and do nothing about it, taking no responsibility at all. It was easy to see that everyone else on the subway felt irritated too. So finally, with what I felt was unusual patience and restraint, I turned to him and said, "Sir, your children are really disturbing a lot of people. I wonder if you couldn't control them a little more?"

The man lifted his gaze as if coming to a consciousness of the situation for the first time and said softly, "Oh, you're right.

125

I guess I should do something about it. We just came from the hospital where their mother died about an hour ago. I don't know what to think, and I guess they don't know how to handle it either."

Can you imagine what I felt at that moment? My paradigm shifted. Suddenly I saw things differently, I felt differently, I behaved differently. My irritation vanished. I didn't have to worry about controlling my attitude or my behavior; my heart was filled with the man's pain. Feelings of sympathy and compassion flowed freely. "Your wife just died? Oh, I'm so sorry. Can you tell me about it? What can I do to help?" Everything changed in an instant.[7]

~

Center your life on principles. Principles don't react to anything. They won't divorce us or run away with our best friend. They aren't out to get us. They can't pave our way with shortcuts and quick fixes. They don't depend on the behavior of others, the environment, or the current fad for their validity. Principles don't die. They aren't here one day and gone the next.[7]

~

Correct principles are like compasses: They are always pointing the way. And if we know how to read them, we won't get lost, confused, or fooled by conflicting voices and values.[19]

⁊

I believe that there are parts to human nature that cannot be reached by either legislation or education, but require the power of God to deal with.[7]

⁊

If I think I see the world as it is, why would I want to value differences in viewpoint? Why would I even want to bother with someone who's "off track"? My paradigm is that I am objective; I see the world as it is. Everyone else is buried in minutiae, but I see the larger picture. That's why they call me a supervisor—I have super vision.[7]

⁊

Management buzzwords are like cotton candy, which tastes good for a second and then evaporates.[8]

⁊

Our perceptions can be vastly different. And yet we live with our mental paradigms for years, thinking they are "facts," and questioning the character or the mental competence of anyone who can't "see the facts." [7]

𝒥𝒫

Our problems and pain are universal and increasing, and the solutions to the problems are and always will be based upon universal, timeless, self-evident principles common to every enduring, prospering society throughout history.[7]

𝒥𝒫

Principles are a part of every major enduring religion, as well as enduring social philosophies and ethical systems. They are self-evident and can easily be validated by any individual.[7]

𝒥𝒫

The character ethic is based on the fundamental idea that there are principles that govern human effectiveness—natural laws in the human dimension that are just as real, just as unchanging and unarguably "there" as laws such as gravity are in the physical dimension.[7]

𝒥𝒫

The way we see the problem is the problem.[7]

∽

There really is a set of values, a sense of fairness, honesty, respect, and contribution that transcends culture—something that is timeless, which transcends the ages and is also self-evident.[8]

∽

Too many human-relations formulas are sunshine philosophies, which sound simple and logical and do work when environmental conditions are freed of the "storms of life." But unless they work on the roots, deep within the character structure of an individual, they only temporarily tranquilize and anesthetize.[4]

∽

Too often we fail to recognize when we're confronting a false dilemma—which is too bad, because in fact most dilemmas are false.[5]

∽

We must look at the lens through which we see the world, as well as the world we see, for the lens shapes how we interpret the world.[7]

ഗ൪

—We see the world, not as it is, but as we are—or as we are conditioned to see it.[7]

ഗ൪

When we open our mouths to describe what we see, we in effect describe ourselves, our perceptions, our paradigms.[7]

ഗ൪

While practices are situationally specific, principles are deep, fundamental truths that have universal application.[7]

ഗ൪

THE
PRINCIPLE
OF
VISION

In your mind's eye, see yourself going to the funeral parlor or chapel, parking the car, and getting out. As you walk inside the building, you notice the flowers, the soft organ music. You see the faces of friends and family you pass along the way. You feel the shared sorrow of losing, the joy of having known, that radiates from the hearts of the people there.

As you walk down to the front of the room and look inside the casket, you suddenly come face to face with yourself. This is your funeral, three years from today. All these people have come to honor you, to express feelings of love and appreciation for your life.

As you take a seat and wait for the services to begin, you look at the program in your hand. There are to be four speakers. The first one is from your family, immediate and also extended—children, brothers, sisters, nephews, nieces, aunts, uncles, cousins, and grandparents who have come from all over the country to attend. The second speaker is one of your friends, someone who can give a sense of what you were as a person. The third speaker is from your work or profession. And the fourth is from your church or some community organization where you've been involved in service.

Now think deeply: What would you like each of these

*speakers to say about you and your life? What kind of husband,
wife, father, or mother would you like their words to reflect?
What kind of son or daughter or cousin? What kind of friend?
What kind of working associate?*

*What character would you like them to have seen in you?
What contributions, what achievements would you want them
to remember? Look carefully at the people around you. What
difference would you like to have made in their lives?*[7]

๑๏

A personal mission statement based on correct principles
becomes a personal constitution, the basis for making
major, life-directing decisions, the basis for making daily
decisions in the midst of the circumstances and emotions
that affect our lives. It empowers individuals with timeless
strength in the midst of change.[7]

๑๏

Begin with the end in mind.[7]

๑๏

Being is seeing in the human dimension.[7]

๑๏

How different our lives are when we really know what is deeply important to us; and keeping that picture in mind, we manage ourselves each day to be and to do what really matters most.[7]

✧

If the ladder is not leaning against the right wall, every step we take just gets us to the wrong place faster.[7]

✧

In building a house, before we turn a shovel of earth we plan almost to the last detail the entire house in our minds, and this is reduced to a blueprint. Therefore, I raise the question: Why should we not also create each day or each week or each year in our minds before we live them in fact?[4]

✧

I can change. I can live out of my imagination instead of my memory. I can tie myself to my limitless potential instead of my limiting past.[7]

✧

Motivation is a fire from within. If someone else tries to light that fire under you, chances are it will burn very briefly.[21]

⚉

The core of any family is what is changeless, what is going to be there—shared vision and values.[7]

⚉

The Knowledge Age we're moving into will outproduce the Industrial Age fifty times—not twice, not three or ten times, but fifty.[8]

⚉

There is no future in a job. The only future is inside yourself.[21]

⚉

There's no way to go for a win in our own lives if we don't even know, in a deep sense, what constitutes a win—what is, in fact, harmonious with our innermost values.[7]

⚉

Through imagination, we can visualize the uncreated worlds of potential that lie within us.[7]

৶

To change ourselves effectively, we first have to change our perceptions.[21]

৶

THE
PRINCIPLE
OF
WIN-WIN

I worked with the leader of a large chain of retail stores who was a bit of a skeptic. "Stephen, this win-win idea sounds good, but it is so idealistic. The tough, realistic business world isn't like that. There's win-lose everywhere, and if you're not out there playing the game, you just can't make it."

"All right," I said, "try going for win-lose with your customers. Is that realistic?"

"Well, no," he replied.

"Why not?"

"I'd lose my customers."

"Then go for lose-win—give the store away. Is that realistic?"

"No. No margin, no mission."

As we considered the various alternatives, win-win appeared to be the only truly realistic approach.

"I guess that's true with customers," he admitted, "but not with suppliers."

"You are the customer of the supplier," I said. "Why doesn't the same principle apply?"

"Well, we recently renegotiated our lease agreements with the mall operators and owners," he said. "We went in with a win-win attitude. We were open, reasonable, conciliatory. But *they saw that position as being soft and weak, and they took us to the cleaners."*

"Well, why did you go for lose-win?" I asked.

"We didn't. We went for win-win."

"I thought you said they took you to the cleaners."

"They did."

"In other words, you lost."

"That's right."

"And they won."

"That's right."

"So what's that called?"

When he realized that what he had called win-win was really lose-win, he was shocked.[7]

❧

Essential to win-win thinking is the Abundance Mentality, the paradigm that there is plenty out there and enough to spare for everybody. It results in sharing of prestige, of recognition, of profits, of decision making. It opens possibilities, options, alternatives, and creativity. The Abundance Mentality flows out of a deep inner sense of personal worth and security.[7]

❧

Even though every job has its monotonous, challengeless aspects, all of us have abundant opportunity somewhere, sometime in our lives to expand our interests, deepen our knowledge and understanding of those interests, and develop our skills and our abilities to participate actively in and to promote those interests—in short, to become "involved in life."[4]

∾

In the long run, if it isn't a win for both of us, we both lose. That's why win-win is the only real alternative in interdependent realities.[7]

∾

Most of life is not a competition. We don't have to live each day competing with our spouse, our children, our co-workers, our neighbors, and our friends. "Who's winning in your marriage?" is a ridiculous question. If both people aren't winning, both are losing.[7]

∾

Most people tend to think in terms of dichotomies: strong or weak, hardball or softball, win or lose. But that kind of thinking is fundamentally flawed. It's based on power and position rather than on principle. Win-win is based on the paradigm that there is plenty for everybody, that one person's success is not achieved at the expense or exclusion of the success of others.[7]

জ৳

Perhaps a sense of possessing needs to come before a sense of genuine sharing.[7]

জ৳

Revenge is a two-edged sword. I know of a divorce in which the husband was directed by the judge to sell the assets and turn over half the proceeds to his exwife. In compliance, he sold a car worth over $10,000 for $50 and gave $25 to the wife.[7]

জ৳

The first thing many people think about when they get into trouble is suing someone, taking him to court, "winning" at someone else's expense. But defensive minds are neither creative nor cooperative.[7]

জ৳

The Scarcity Mentality is the zero-sum paradigm of life. Often, people with a Scarcity Mentality harbor secret hopes that others might suffer misfortune—not terrible misfortune, but acceptable misfortune that would keep them "in their place." Their sense of self-worth comes from being compared to others; and someone else's success, to some degree, means their failure.[7]

⁂

The win-win mentality is fundamental not just to business but to all of life's relationships. It's the ticket to entry into any human being's heart.[5]

⁂

Think win-win.[7]

⁂

We often assume that the whole point of an argument is to win—to beat the other side. Just try that on your friends and family and see how far you get toward a loving and creative relationship.[5]

⁂

Winning is fun. But there is more than one way to win. Life isn't a tennis game in which only one player gets to jump the net. It's even more exciting when both sides win, when they create a new reality that delights them both.[5]

જ઼ઽ

Win-win is not a personality technique. Win-win is a frame of mind and heart that constantly seeks mutual benefit in all human interactions. It's a total philosophy of human interaction. It comes from a character of integrity, maturity, and the Abundance Mentality. It grows out of high-trust relationships.[7]

જ઼ઽ

STEPHEN R. COVEY'S
FAVORITE
QUOTATIONS

We are what we repeatedly do. Excellence, then, is not an act, but a habit.

—Aristotle

ↄ℗

Sow a thought, and you reap an act;
Sow an act, and you reap a habit;
Sow a habit, and you reap a character;
Sow a character, and you reap a destiny.

—Attributed to George Dana Boardman

ↄ℗

The child must know that he is a miracle, that since the beginning of the world there hasn't been, and until the end of the world there will not be, another child like him.

—Pablo Casals

ↄ℗

Plans are worthless; but planning is invaluable.

—Peter Drucker

∽

The significant problems we face cannot be solved at the same level of thinking we were at when we created them.

—Attributed to Albert Einstein

∽

The history of free man is never written by chance but by choice—their choice.

—Dwight D. Eisenhower

∽

We shall not cease from exploration
And the end of all our exploring
Will be to arrive where we started
And know the place for the first time.

—T. S. Eliot

∽

That which we persist in doing becomes easier—not that the nature of the task has changed, but our ability to do it has increased.

—Ralph Waldo Emerson

All children are born geniuses: 9,999 out of every 10,000 are swiftly, inadvertently de-geniusized by grownups.

—Buckminster Fuller

Things which matter most must never be at the mercy of things which matter least.

—Johann Wolfgang von Goethe

Treat a man as he is and he will remain as he is. Treat a man as he can and should be and he will become as he can and should be.

—Johann Wolfgang von Goethe

The successful person has the habit of doing the things failures don't like to do. They don't like doing them either necessarily. But their disliking is subordinated to the strength of their purpose.

—E. M. Gray

It is more noble to give yourself completely to one individual than to labor diligently for the salvation of the masses.

—Dag Hammarskjöld

I wouldn't give a fig for the simplicity on the near side of complexity; but I would give my right arm for the simplicity on the far side of complexity.

—Oliver Wendell Holmes

What lies behind us and what lies before us are tiny matters compared to what lies within us.

—Oliver Wendell Holmes

There can be no friendship without confidence, and no confidence without integrity.

—Samuel Johnson

I am constantly amazed by two things: the starry heavens above and the moral law within.

—Immanuel Kant

Every half-truth at length produces the contradiction of itself in the opposite half-truth.

—D. H. Lawrence

The dogmas of the quiet past are inadequate to the stormy present.

—Abraham Lincoln

I have so much to do today, I'll need to spend another hour on my knees.

—Attributed to Martin Luther

ↈ

Habits are like a cable: We weave a strand of it every day and soon it cannot be broken.

—Horace Mann

ↈ

We have committed the Golden Rule to memory; let us now commit it to life.

—Edwin Markham

ↈ

The greatest battles of life are fought out every day in the silent chambers of one's own soul.

—David O. McKay

ↈ

If there are any persons who contest a received opinion, let us thank them for it, open our minds to listen to them, and rejoice that there is someone to do for us what we otherwise ought.

—John Stuart Mill

When I look back on my life nowadays, which I some-times do, what strikes me most forcibly about it is that what seemed at the time most significant and seductive, seems now most futile and absurd.

—Malcolm Muggeridge

That which we obtain too easily, we esteem too lightly. It is dearness only which gives everything its value. Heaven knows how to put a proper price on its goods.

—Thomas Paine

The heart has its reasons which reason knows not of.

—Blaise Pascal

No one can hurt you without your consent.

—Eleanor Roosevelt

୶୦

It is the weak who are cruel. Gentleness can only be expected from the strong.

—Leo Roskin

୶୦

This is the true joy in life—the being used for a purpose recognized by yourself as a mighty one; the being a force of nature, instead of a feverish, selfish little clod of ailments and grievances complaining that the world will not devote itself to making you happy. I am of the opinion that my life belongs to the whole community, and as long as I live it is my privilege to do for it whatever I can. I want to be thoroughly used up when I die. For the harder I work the more I live. I rejoice in life for its own sake. Life is no brief candle to me. It's a sort of splendid torch which I've got to hold up for the moment, and I want to make it burn as brightly as possible before handing it on to future generations.

—George Bernard Shaw

୶୦

We are not human beings having a spiritual experience. We are spiritual beings having a human experience.

—Pierre Teilhard de Chardin

✑

Give the world the best you have and you may get hurt.
Give the world your best anyway.
                                        —Mother Teresa

✑

I know of no more encouraging fact than the unquestion-
able ability of man to elevate his life by conscious endeavor.
                                        —Henry David Thoreau

✑

There are a thousand hacking at the branches of evil to one
who is striking at the root.
                                        —Henry David Thoreau

✑

REFERENCE LIST

BOOKS BY STEPHEN R. COVEY

1. *First Things First: To Live, to Love, to Learn, to Leave a Legacy* (New York: Simon & Schuster, 1995).
2. *Great Work, Great Career* (Salt Lake City: FranklinCovey Co., 2010).
3. *Principle-Centered Leadership* (New York: Simon & Schuster, 1991).
4. *Spiritual Roots of Human Relations* (Salt Lake City: Deseret Book, 1976).
5. *The 3rd Alternative: Solving Life's Most Difficult Problems* (New York: Free Press, 2011).
6. *The 7 Habits of Highly Effective Families* (New York: St. Martin's Griffin, 1997).
7. *The 7 Habits of Highly Effective People* (New York: Free Press, 2004).
8. *The 8th Habit: From Effectiveness to Greatness* (New York: Free Press, 2004).
9. *The Leader in Me* (New York: Free Press, 2008).

OTHER SOURCES

10. "Big Rocks," FranklinCovey video, 1989.
11. B. J. Gallagher, "Why Don't I Do the Things I Know Are Good for Me?" (New York: Penguin, 2009).
12. Janet Attwood and Jack Canfield, "Dr. Stephen R. Covey, Leading People from Effectiveness to Greatness," *A Life on Fire: Living Your Life With Passion, Balance, and Abundance* (Enlightened Alliances, LLC, no date).
13. "Knowledge Workers: 10,000 Times the Productivity." Stephen R. Covey blog. http://www.stephencovey.com/blog?p=15.
14. "Dr. Stephen Covey Interview Featuring Jay Abraham, May 10, 2005." http://abraham-pop.s3.amazonaws.com/stephencoveyinterview.pdf.
15. "Our Children and the Crisis in Education," *Huffington Post*, April 20, 2010. http://www.huffingtonpost.com/stephen-r-covey/our-children-and-the-cris?_B_545034.html.
16. Leo Babauta, "Exclusive Interview: Stephen Covey on His Morning Routine, Technology, Blogs, GTD and The Secret." http://zenhabits.net/exclusive-interview-stephen-covey-on-his-morning-routine-blogs-technology-gtd-and-the-secret/.
17. Dan Schawbel, "Stephen Covey Gives You a 3rd Alternative," *Forbes*, Oct. 4, 2011. http://www.forbes.com/sites/danschawbel/2011/10/04/stephen-r-covey-gives-you-a-3rd-alternative/.
18. Stephen R. Covey, "We Can Do Better Than This: A 3rd Alternative," *Huffington Post*, October 6, 2011. http://www.huffingtonpost.com/stephen-r-covey/we-can-do-bette-than-thi_2_b_998107.html.
19. "A Day With Stephen Covey," July 17, 2012. http://insights.execunet.com/index.php/comments/a_day_with_stephen_r_covey/best-practices/more.
20. Personal conversation with Stephen R. Covey.
21. Unsourced, attributed to Stephen R. Covey.

ABOUT THE AUTHOR

Stephen R. Covey, one of *Time* magazine's twenty-five most influential Americans, dedicated his life to demonstrating with profound yet straightforward guidance how every person can control his or her destiny. He was an internationally respected leadership authority, family expert, teacher, organizational consultant, and author. He sold over 20 million books (in 40 languages), and *The 7 Habits of Highly Effective People* was named the #1 Most Influential Business Book of the 20th Century. His other bestselling books include *Principle-Centered Leadership, First Things First, The 7 Habits of Highly Effective Families, The 8th Habit: From Effectiveness to Greatness,* and *The Leader in Me: How Schools and Parents Around the World Are Inspiring Greatness One Child at a Time.* He was the cofounder of FranklinCovey, a leading global education and training firm with offices in 147 countries. A popular professor and administrator for many years at Brigham Young University, Dr. Covey also held the Jon M. Huntsman Presidential Chair in Leadership at Utah State University. He lived with his wife and family in Utah.